Savannah
SCAVENGER
HUNT

Savannah SCAVENGER HUNT

WRITTEN AND PHOTOGRAPHED BY
CHRIS SERGI

PELICAN PUBLISHING COMPANY
GRETNA 2016

The word "Pelican" and the depiction of a pelican are
trademarks of Pelican Publishing Company, Inc., and are
registered in the U.S. Patent and Trademark Office.

Library of Congress Cataloging-in-Publication Data

Sergi, Chris.
  Savannah scavenger hunt / written and photographed by Chris
Sergi.
      pages cm
  Includes index.
  ISBN 978-1-4556-2152-1 (paperback : alkaline paper) — ISBN
978-1-4556-2153-8 (e-book) 1. Savannah (Ga.)—Guidebooks.
2. Savannah (Ga.)—Buildings, structures, etc.—Guidebooks. 3.
Historic sites—Georgia—Savannah—Guidebooks. I. Title.
  F294.S2S46 2016
  917.58'72404--dc23
                          2015035845

Printed in the United States of America
Published by Pelican Publishing Company, Inc.
1000 Burmaster Street, Gretna, Louisiana 70053

To my children, who were a great help and inspiration in creating this book

Contents

Introduction

This book was designed for all ages to enjoy and discover the City of Savannah and surrounding areas. We have so many visitors coming here every year, and half of those are families. Also, Savannah is a fast-growing city, with many college students and families wanting to learn about their new surroundings in the Low Country. I wanted to create a book that would be fun and engage all ages, from the smallest child who can't yet read but can look at the photographs and get excited about the finds, to the older child or adult who enjoys the game and doesn't even realize how much he or she is learning about the history of Georgia and the founding of our country.

If you are visiting Savannah, or just looking for something fun to do with friends or family, *Savannah Scavenger Hunt* is a great way to explore the city and its history, while making wonderful memories that will last forever.

Savannah
SCAVENGER
HUNT

Historic Downtown Savannah

Historic Downtown Savannah

Savannah was the first colony of Georgia, founded on February 12, 1733, by Gen. James Edward Oglethorpe. He sailed from England with 120 passengers on the good ship *Anne*. Oglethorpe chose the site for its high bluff overlooking the Savannah River. He named the thirteenth American colony "Georgia," after King George II. Savannah was the first state capital of Georgia. The word "Savannah" means flat, grassy plain. In the beginning, it was a military colony, acting as a buffer between South Carolina and the Spaniards in Florida. Savannah was also founded so England could send its poor and unemployed to the New World to work for their mother country. The original seal of Georgia reads, in Latin, *Not for themselves but for others.* Savannah is also known as one of America's first planned cities. General Oglethorpe laid it out in twenty-four squares, today known as the "Jewels of the City." The nation's largest National Landmark Historic District, Savannah is famous for its rich history, cobblestone streets, lush gardens, canopies of live oak trees, detailed ironwork, and beautiful architecture. This city has so many hidden treasures just waiting to be found.

Let's get started!

Here is a map of Historic Downtown Savannah to help you find your way.

Good luck, and happy hunting!

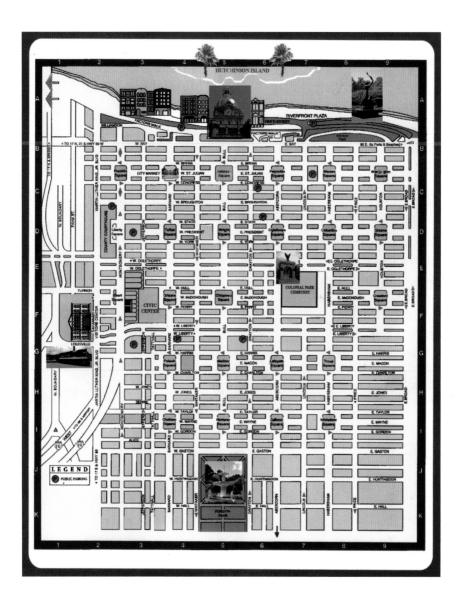

It doesn't matter where you start or where you end, as long as you have fun!

Savannah is known as the "Hospitality City of the South." Pineapples are the symbol for hospitality. Christopher Columbus brought the fruit back to Europe in 1496. The Spaniards soon learned they were welcome in a village if a pineapple was placed by the entrance. This symbolism spread to Europe, then to colonial North America, and is still used today. Did you know that Spanish moss is a relative of the pineapple? The plant absorbs nutrients and water from the air and can grow in many different kinds of trees. If it has fallen to the ground, it may have small insects in it called "chiggers" or "red bugs." So be careful when handling it!

How many pineapples can you find in Savannah?

You can start anywhere, but it's always fun to end your scavenger hunt at Leopold's Ice Cream to celebrate your discoveries!

Leopold's has been a Savannah tradition since 1919 and is a favorite. They still use the old recipes that they have perfected over the years and that people have come to love! Johnny Mercer, the famous singer and songwriter who grew up in Savannah, even wrote a song about Leopold's signature flavor, tutti-frutti.

1. Forsyth Park Fountain

This fountain was erected in 1858 as the centerpiece of Forsyth Park. William Hodgson, husband of Mary Telfair, donated ten acres for the park for the "pleasure of the public." It is named for Georgia governor John Forsyth, who donated an additional twenty acres, known as the parade grounds. In the middle of those grounds is the Confederate Monument, erected in 1874. The soldier is facing North, guarding the South.

Can you find the soldier facing North?

Bonus Finds

➤ The Fragrant Garden in Forsyth Park was dedicated in 1963 for the blind to enjoy. Hint: Look behind the playground on the west side of the park.

➤ Three fauns hold up a bench in the Fragrant Garden.

2. The Twin Steeples of the Cathedral of Saint John the Baptist

This French Gothic cathedral on Lafayette Square was begun in 1873. It is the Mother Church of the Catholic Diocese of Savannah. In the beginning, Catholics were prohibited from settling in the colony because it was feared they would sympathize with the Catholic Spaniards in neighboring Florida. The Sisters of Mercy came to Savannah in 1845 and established St. Vincent's Academy, which is still in use today.

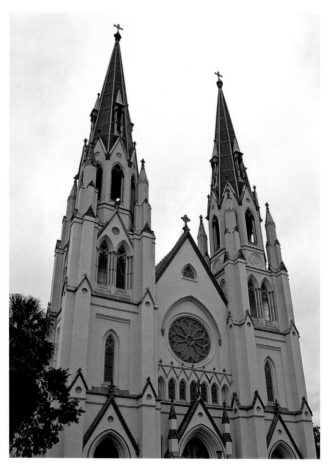

Bonus Finds

➤ A stained-glass window of Saint Patrick is located inside the cathedral. Savannah has one of the largest Saint Patrick's Day parades in the U.S.

➤ Saint Denis was beheaded but picked up his head and kept walking. This scene is depicted in the cathedral.

➤ Saint Joan of Arc was a heroine of France. She is shown in the cathedral in her armor.

3. The Andrew Low House

This home, which presides over Lafayette Square, was built in 1848 by New York architect John Norris. Andrew Low was a wealthy cotton factor and father of William Mackay Low, who married Juliette Gordon. Juliette Gordon Low

would found the Girl Scouts of America. In this house, the charter for the Girl Scouts was signed on March 12, 1912. Today it is owned by the Colonial Dames of Georgia and serves as their state headquarters. The Carriage House is owned by the Girl Scouts and was their first headquarters. The front garden still follows the original hourglass arrangement designed by the architect. Gen. Robert E. Lee was a guest in the home, as well as English author William Makepeace Thackeray.

Bonus Finds

➤ Guarding the front steps of the Andrew Low House are one of Juliette Gordon Low's favorite features of the home, these lazy lions.

4. The Armillary Sphere in Troup Square

Troup Square was laid out in 1851 and named for George Michael Troup, a U.S. senator from Georgia. The Armillary Sphere in the center, supported by six tortoises, represents an ancient astronomical device. Savannah holds its Blessing of the Animals in Troup Square every year.

Can you find all six tortoises?

Bonus Finds

➤ The Unitarian Universalist Church, also known as the "Jingle Bells" Church, was built in 1851 on Oglethorpe Square but moved after the Civil War to Troup Square. James L. Pierpont was the music director for the church in the 1850s and wrote the music and lyrics for "Jingle Bells," originally naming it "The One-Horse Open Sleigh." He composed many songs over the years, but "Jingle Bells" has always been the most popular.

5. Monument to Sgt. William Jasper

Sgt. William Jasper bravely saved the colors in several battles, including the 1779 Battle of Savannah during the Revolutionary War. In this monument in Madison Square, one hand holds the flag, and the other presses the wound where he has just been shot. The panels around the memorial tell how he died in that battle. This monument was unveiled on George Washington's birthday in 1883. Madison Square was named in honor of the fourth president of the U.S., James Madison.

Bonus Finds

➤ A lion may be seen on the Scottish Rite Temple. Hyman Witcover designed and constructed this unique building in 1916. Hint: Look above the entrance to the temple.

➤ Gargoyles may be seen on the steeple of Saint John's Episcopal Church. Calvin Otis of New York designed the Gothic-style church. The cornerstone was laid in March 1852.

➤ Cannons are attached to the Savannah Volunteer Guards Armory, built by William Preston in 1892.

6. Canopy of Live Oak Trees Over Jones Street

This street was named in honor of Mayor John Jones, who also died fighting in the Battle of Savannah in 1779. The brick street is lined with live oak trees, Georgia's state tree, and they are draped with Spanish moss. Mrs. Wilkes' Dining Room, at the corner of Whitaker Street, is another Savannah tradition, since 1943.

Bonus Finds

➤ Jones Street is known for its mansions and row houses dating from the mid- to late 1850s.

➤ There are also many beautiful hidden gardens located there.

7. Massie School

Built on Calhoun Square in 1856 by John Norris, this was the first public elementary school in Georgia. Students started each day with a prayer, and testing was advertised in the newspaper as a public event. During the Civil War, the building was used as a Federal hospital, but later, it resumed classes. Massie School closed in 1974 but today serves as a museum.

Bonus Finds

➤ Calhoun Square was named for John C. Calhoun of South Carolina, who as secretary of war visited Savannah in 1819. There are many beautiful gardens to find around Calhoun Square, but *please* be respectful, as they are private property. How many hidden gardens can you find?

8. Congregation Mickve Israel

This is the third oldest Jewish congregation in the country. When the Jewish settlers arrived, the colony's trustees did not want to grant them land. Oglethorpe defied the trustees and gave the settlers fifty acres each. His decision was influenced by Samuel Nunez, a Jewish doctor who stopped an epidemic that had already killed twenty of the original colonists. This synagogue dates to 1878 and is said to be the only Gothic-style Jewish temple in the country. Monterey Square was laid out in 1847 and named to honor a battle that year in the Mexican War in which the U.S. captured the city of Monterrey, Mexico.

Bonus Finds

➤ Iron posts of noble pelicans guard each side of the main-entrance stairs to a nearby residence. As Savannah is a port city, many different examples of marine motifs may be found in its architecture and ironwork. Hint: Look on the northwest corner of Taylor Street and Bull Street.

➤ Gen. Casimir Pulaski was a famous Polish patriot during the Revolutionary War. He died as a "Freedom Fighter" in 1779 at the Siege of Savannah, fighting for American independence and his love of liberty. Can you find his monument?

9. Colonial Park Cemetery

This graveyard was established in 1750 as the burial ground for the parish of Christ Church. In 1789, it was expanded for all denominations, but with the many epidemics and wars in Savannah, by 1850 the cemetery was full and closed to all burials. Famous people interred here include:

➤ Button Gwinnett, who signed the Declaration of Independence (very few original examples of his signature exist)
➤ Gen. Lachlan McIntosh, a Revolutionary War hero who killed Gwinnett in a duel in 1777
➤ William Scarbrough, one of the principal owners of the first steamship to cross the Atlantic Ocean
➤ Joseph Habersham, postmaster general of the United States

➤ Archibald Bulloch, great-great-grandfather of Pres. Theodore Roosevelt.

During the Civil War, Union troops occupying Savannah used the cemetery for their stables and camping grounds.

The Daughters of the American Revolution erected the DAR Patriots Arch in 1913 to memorialize the Revolutionary War veterans buried here.

Bonus Finds

➤ This headstone with a skull and crossbones was one of many that were destroyed during the Civil War. Union troops not happy about spending Christmas and New Year's Eve camped out in this Southern cemetery damaged tombstones and altered some of the ages and dates in 1864. The skull and crossbones symbolize mortality. Hint: Look midway down the brick wall at the back of the cemetery.

➤ Button Gwinnett's monument bears an image of the signature he placed on the Declaration of Independence.

➤ Look for a snake in the shape of a circle. It symbolizes the circle of life: no beginning and no end.

10. The Owens-Thomas House

William Jay built this home on Oglethorpe Square for Richard Richardson in 1819 at a cost of $50,000. It is considered the first and finest example of Regency architecture in America. The house features a bridge on the second floor, curved walls, a Greek-key window in the dining room, and a rounded ceiling in the drawing room. It was also one of the first homes in America to have indoor plumbing. In 1830, the house was purchased by Savannah politician George W. Owens and remained in his family for the next 121 years. When his granddaughter Margaret Gray Thomas died, she willed the home and furnishings to the Telfair Museum, to be opened to the public and to honor her father and grandfather. It opened in 1954 as the first house museum in Savannah. In March of 1825, the Marquis de Lafayette stayed two nights in the home during his tour of the United States, so it is now on the National Register of Historic Places.

Bonus Finds

➤ This cast-iron balcony represents the first use of structural ironwork in America. The Marquis de Lafayette addressed the City of Savannah from this balcony in 1825.

➤ The nearby orange-tree gate is a wonderful example of wrought iron in Savannah. Hint: Look for it at 123 Habersham Street.

11. Columbia Square Fountain

This decorative cast-iron fountain resembles a tree trunk with leaves, ferns, vines, flowers, and even frogs. It was moved from Wormsloe Plantation to Columbia Square in 1970. The plantation was owned by Noble Jones, who came over with James Oglethorpe on the ship *Anne*. Jones became the most prosperous of the early colonists, owning 7,000 acres of land. Columbia Square was laid out in 1799 and named after the popular nickname for the American colonies.

Bonus Finds

➤ Cast-iron frogs hide on the Columbia Square Fountain. How many can you find?

12. The Davenport House

Isaiah Davenport built this elegant home on Columbia Square for his family in 1820. The house is a good example of Federal-style architecture in America. When it was threatened with demolition in 1955, seven ladies led by Anna Hunter raised the money to save the home and created the Historic Savannah Foundation. In 1963, the Davenport House became a museum, and it is now on the National Register of Historic Places.

Bonus Finds

➤ The Davenport House's English Garden is a replica of an eighteenth-century garden and a site for weddings, parties, and even period reenactments such as "Tea at Mrs. Davenport's."

13. The Pirate's House

This location on East Broad Street near East Bay Street was the site of Trustees Garden, the first experimental garden in America. William Houston was a traveling botanist employed by the English to search for plants that would grow in Georgia. The English were hoping to raise mulberry trees, essential to the culture of silk, but they only produced eight pounds of silk. Queen Charlotte had a dress made from it. An inn for sailors was later constructed on the garden. When pirates arrived at the new colony, they dug tunnels under this building for easy access to the river and their ships. They even built a large rum cellar under a chamber known as the "Captain's Room." The Pirate's House was a favorite spot for the fictional Captain Flint from *Treasure Island*, and it is believed that the attic was the setting for his death. The Pirate's House is a restaurant today and a popular tourist attraction.

Bonus Finds

➤ The Herb House is considered to be one of the oldest buildings in the state of Georgia, dating to the 1730s.

➤ Pirates used the tunnels below the Pirate's House as secret passageways to bring in their treasure and get to their ships quickly, if needed. *Beware!*

14. Florence Martus, "The Waving Girl"

Florence Martus was born on Cockspur Island on August 7, 1868. She was the daughter of John H. Martus, stationed at Fort Pulaski. She started waving at all ships entering or leaving the port at the age of nineteen, in 1887. She moved in with her brother George W. Martus, a lighthouse keeper on Elba Island, and lived there until he retired in 1931. For forty-four years, she never missed greeting a single ship. By day she would wave a handkerchief, and at night her dog would wake her and she would wave a lantern. Many stories say she was looking for a lost love, but she denied it until her

death in 1943. Look for her famous statue on the riverfront.

As you walk along River Street, notice the old cotton warehouses dating from the 1790s to 1840s. They span the bluff and are some of Savannah's most unique architectural features.

Bonus Finds

➤ There is an "Echo Spot" marked by an *X*. Try it! Stand in the middle of the *X* and say something. You'll hear an echo. Hint: Look across from 313 East River Street.

➤ To find the Sandbox Tugboat, look halfway down River Street, across from River Street Sweets.

15. Savannah's City Hall

The city hall was built on the spot where Gen. James Oglethorpe landed in 1733 and where the old City Exchange building stood, from 1799 to 1904. Hyman Witcover constructed it in 1906, at a cost of $205,167, using granite and limestone. The two statues over the entrance represent art and commerce. The original copper dome was covered in gold in 1987. This is the second gold dome in the state of Georgia; Atlanta has the first.

Bonus Finds

➤ In 1791, George Washington visited Savannah on his Southern tour. He was met by John Houston, Savannah's first mayor. Washington was honored with many parties, dances, and a dinner for 200 people on the river, complete with fireworks. To thank the City of Savannah for its hospitality, he sent these cannons, the "Washington Guns," which were captured at the Battle of Yorktown during the Revolutionary War.

➤ The griffin is a mythical creature said to guard one's fortune. William Preston designed and built this terra-cotta fountain, along with the Cotton Exchange, in the 1880s. Cotton was Savannah's "fortune" at that time.

16. Monument to Nathanael Greene

The Marquis de Lafayette laid the cornerstone of this memorial in 1825 to honor Nathanael Greene, a Revolutionary War hero and second in command under George Washington. The state of Georgia gratefully awarded him with Mulberry Grove Plantation after the war. Years later, his wife, Catharine, hired Eli Whitney to educate their children at Mulberry Grove, and he invented the cotton gin there. Greene and his son were buried under this monument. Johnson Square was the first square laid out in Savannah and is known as the "Keystone Square." It was named for Robert Johnson, royal governor of South Carolina.

Bonus Finds

➤ Christ Church Episcopal is the Mother Church of Georgia and was originally Anglican. James Hamilton built the church you see today in 1838. This is where Juliette Gordon Low, founder of the Girl Scouts of America, married Andrew Low's only son, William Mackay Low, on the anniversary of her parents' wedding on December 21, 1886.

17. The First African Baptist Church

Slaves built this church in 1859 in the little spare time they had. Runaway slaves were hidden under the church; patterns of holes were placed in the floorboards so that they could have air. This church was part of the Underground Railroad, a network of secret routes and safe houses used by African slaves to escape to free states. They painted decorative symbols of their African heritage on some of the pews in the balcony. The stained-glass windows over the main altar depict early ministers of the church. Franklin Square was named for Benjamin Franklin, who was an agent for Georgia in London.

Bonus Finds

➤ Ellis Square was one of the original four squares laid out in 1733. It was named for Henry Ellis, the second royal governor of Georgia. This interactive fountain is a good find on a hot day!

➤ Paula Deen's Lady and Sons Restaurant, opened in 1996, is one of her original restaurants. It's a great find for lunch!

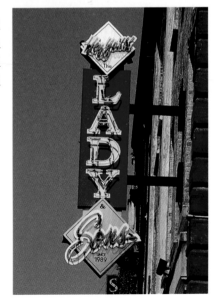

18. Telfair Art Museum

William Jay designed this house in 1819 for Alexander Telfair, who was on the board of the United States Bank. He passed it down to his daughter Mary Telfair, who willed it to the Georgia Historical Society in 1876. The house was to be open to the public as Telfair Academy of Arts and Sciences.

Telfair Square is one of the original four squares laid out in 1733. Originally named St. James Square, it was renamed in 1883 to honor Edward Telfair, three-time governor of Georgia.

Bonus Finds

➤ The Jepson Center, Telfair's contemporary art museum, opened in 2006. It has over 7,500 square feet of gallery space, including ArtZeum, a great interactive art gallery for families.

➤ In Telfair Square is a tribute to the Girl Scouts of America. Hint: Look for a marker in the southeast corner.

19. Tomochichi's Grave and the Gordon Monument

Wright Square, named for James Wright, the last royal governor of Georgia, was also called "Courthouse Square," from the early days when it had the first courthouse in the colony. Tomochichi, chief of the Yamacraw Indians, signed a "Treaty of Friendship" with James Oglethorpe and was buried in Wright Square in 1739. Tomochichi wanted to be buried among the English in Savannah and was honored with a parade and large funeral service.

There is also a large 1884 monument here to William Washington Gordon, the founder of the Central of Georgia Railroad. Four winged figures on top represent Agriculture, Manufacture, Commerce, and Art. Can you spot them?

Bonus Finds

➤ The Colonial Dames of Georgia placed a boulder of Georgia granite in Wright Square in 1899 in memory of Tomochichi.

➤ Look for a train on the Gordon Monument.

➤ Architect William Aiken built the U.S. Federal Building in 1894. All the different types of marble quarried in Georgia appear at the top. Search for the face on the building.

20. Independent Presbyterian Church Steeple

Scotsmen who landed with Oglethorpe in 1733 founded this church. John Holden Greene was the architect. The church was dedicated in 1819, with Pres. James Monroe in attendance, who was visiting Savannah. It was destroyed by fire in 1889 but rebuilt in 1891 from the original plans, supervised by architect William Preston. The steeple rises 227 feet and is made of cast iron and steel. Woodrow Wilson married Ellen Axson in this church in June of 1885. It is located near Chippewa Square, which was named for a battle in the War of 1812.

Bonus Finds

➤ The Juliette Gordon Low birthplace is a Regency-style townhouse built in 1820. The founder of the Girl Scouts of America was born in this house on Halloween 1860. It was named Savannah's first National Historic Landmark in 1965, and the Girl Scouts of America own and operate it today. It has a beautiful Victorian garden on the side, behind an elegant wrought-iron gate.

➤ Across from Juliette's garden, on the other side of Oglethorpe Avenue, is the "Old" Chatham Academy. Built in 1901, it now houses the Chatham County Board of Public Education. Look up to see "the ladies"!

21. The Monument of Gen. James Edward Oglethorpe

The statue in the center of Chippewa Square honors Gen. James Edward Oglethorpe, the founder of the colony of Georgia. He proudly faces south, guarding South Carolina from the Spaniards in Florida. The monument, by Daniel Chester French, was unveiled in 1910. He also designed the seated Lincoln in Washington, D.C. The figure of Oglethorpe is bronze, with lions on each side holding the different seals of Georgia. The original seal of Georgia had a Latin inscription meaning "Not for themselves but for others."

Bonus Finds

➤ This dolphin downspout by Ivan Bailey is a good example of Savannah's ironwork. Hint: Look at the corner of Bull Street and West Perry Street.

➤ After 1819, this was a popular square. It had the city's first theater, Savannah Theatre, designed by William Jay. It's still a great place for live shows today!

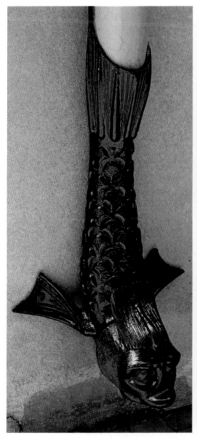

22. Georgia State Railroad Museum

The Central of Georgia Railroad started in 1833 to attract investment capital to the area. It was constructed to connect the Macon and Western Railroad to seaports on the Atlantic coast. It was not completed until 1843. It was headed by William Washington Gordon and very successful; within ten years they had built the longest continuous railroad under one management in the world, measuring 190 miles. The rails brought cotton and other products to Savannah's port. This museum is believed to be the largest antebellum railroad-repair facility in the world. Hint: It is near Louisville Road and Martin Luther King Jr. Boulevard.

Bonus Finds

➤ The Savannah Children's Museum is part of the Georgia State Railroad Museum. It features an Exploration Station and exhibits on math, music, literacy, culture, science, and art.

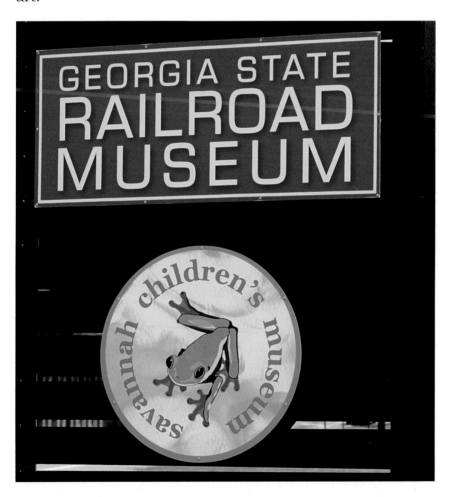

There are so many things to discover in Savannah!

How many things did you find?

What were the hardest finds?

What was your favorite find in the historic district?

On the way to Bonaventure Cemetery there are some more. . . .

Bonus Finds

➤ Victory Drive is part of U.S. Route 80. It runs east-west through midtown Savannah. It is famous for its long line of palm trees, stretching nineteen miles from Ogeechee Road to Tybee Island. There are 360 palm trees, all in honor of those who fought and lost their lives in World War I. In 1919, the City of Savannah decided to make Victory Drive a Memorial Military Boulevard. The Savannah Women's Federation erected a monument in 1929 to all the soldiers killed in World War I. On this monument, located at the corner of Victory Drive and Waters Avenue in Daffin Park, a "Roll of Honor" lists those soldiers.

In the spring, when the azaleas are in bloom, Victory Drive comes alive with color!

How many shrimp boats can you count in Thunderbolt?

Thunderbolt, Georgia is a small town about five miles southeast of downtown Savannah. It is located on the Wilmington River, which is part of the U.S. Intracoastal Waterway. Native Americans first settled Thunderbolt, and when the English colonized Georgia in 1733, the small community became a shipping site for local plantations. In 1856, it developed into a processing port for the fishing community and also serviced the river traffic. Thunderbolt was named for a legend that told of a large bolt of lightning that struck the ground here and created a spring on the Wilmington Bluff. Today, Thunderbolt is an important part of Georgia's shrimping industry and a picturesque and unique town known for its seafood and rich history.

Bonaventure Cemetery

Bonaventure Cemetery

To reach Bonaventure Cemetery from Historic Downtown Savannah, head south on Bull Street.

Then turn right on West Gaston Street. Turn left on Whitaker Street.

You'll go by Forsyth Park.

Keep going down Whitaker Street. Turn left onto Victory Drive and go all the way down to Bonaventure Road.

It will be on the left side of Victory Drive.

Turn left on Bonaventure Road and go down until you see the gates of the cemetery. The address is 330 Bonaventure Road. Bonaventure Cemetery is open from 8:00 to 5:00 daily; the phone number is 912-651-6843.

On this map, the main road through Thunderbolt to Bonaventure Cemetery is marked in yellow. If you keep following Victory Drive, it takes you to Tybee Island.

The History of Bonaventure Cemetery

Bonaventure Cemetery is a beautiful graveyard overlooking the Wilmington River just five miles from downtown Savannah. It was once Bonaventure Plantation. *Bonaventure* is French for "good fortune." Colonel Mulryne built the first house here in 1760. His daughter Mary later married Josiah Tattnall, and the groves of live oak trees were planted in the shape of an *M* and *T* in honor of the two families joining. During the Revolutionary War, the fortunes and property of both families were confiscated when the two men publicly declared their loyalty to the king of England. Bonaventure was the landing site, camping grounds, and hospital for the French during the Siege of Savannah in 1779. After the Revolutionary War, in 1788, Josiah Tattnall, Jr., purchased Bonaventure, returning it to the Tattnall family. In 1847, Josiah Tattnall III sold the 600-acre plantation to Peter Wiltberger for $5,000 to become a public cemetery ground. Tattnall and his family are buried in the cemetery, along with his parents and five siblings. During the Victorian period, death became romanticized as a state of hope and slumber. You can see this reflected throughout Bonaventure Cemetery today, with its elaborate graves and beautiful statues. People enjoy coming to this place to visit their loved ones or view the tombs. They even bring picnics and take long strolls through the cemetery on Sunday afternoons. Today this is still an active cemetery of 100 acres, owned by the City of Savannah. Thanks to the Historical Bonaventure Society, in 2001 Bonaventure was placed on the National Register of Historic Places.

Bonaventure Cemetery is a canopy of live oak trees draped with Spanish moss. It is an enchanted garden full of angels, vaults, and statues of every kind. Be careful . . . it is easy to get lost in the echoes of its past.

Please be respectful of its history and help preserve it for future generations. This is still an active cemetery, so be considerate of the families.

You can easily spend all day here, so you might want to bring a picnic. If you have bikes, it is also great to just park your car at the front and ride around.

Let's get started!

1. The Two Front Gates

Bonaventure Cemetery is divided into two sections, the Christian and the Jewish. Both have their own gates and entranceways. At one, a woman embracing a Christian cross symbolizes faith; it is inscribed: *Simply to the cross I cling.* The Star of David at the other gate is a symbol of Jewish faith and divine protection.

2. The Gaston Tomb

A vault at the entrance of Bonaventure memorializes William Gaston, known to be a wonderful host in Savannah. It was erected to host anyone who died while visiting Savannah until other arrangements could be made. It is inscribed: *Savannah's host to the living and the dead.*

3. The Little Gracie Statue

Another favorite statue honors little Gracie Watson, the only child of W. J. and Frances Watson. He was the manager of the old Pulaski Hotel. Gracie would greet guests and was a favorite among them. When she died of pneumonia at the age of six, her parents were heartbroken and had this very lifelike statue made by John Walz from a photograph of her. You will notice that she is interred here alone. Her parents moved home to New England and were buried there. The people of Savannah promised to watch over Gracie and always have. The ivy that appears on the statue symbolizes friendship, as Gracie was said to be a friend to everyone she met. Hint: Look for this statue in section E.

Bonus Find

➤ Look for the angel with the palm branch. The branch symbolizes peace, victory over death, and eternal life. The cross represents Christianity, and a horizontal cross represents the earth and humanity, the suffering of mankind, an end to suffering, and the resurrection of Jesus. It is also a reminder to Christians to "take up your cross and follow Jesus." This monument is inscribed: *He has laid his cross down and is safe in the arms of the lord.*

4. The Bust of Gen. Robert H. Anderson

General Anderson was born in Savannah in 1835 and graduated from West Point in 1857. He fought in the Civil War and worked his way up to a Confederate brigadier general. General Anderson took part in the Atlanta Campaign and fought in the "March to the Sea." After the war, he came back to Savannah and became chief of police, until his death in 1888.

Bonus Find

➤ Dipping Confederate soldiers' hats, sashes, belts, or swords in bronze was a popular way to honor them. You can find many examples throughout Bonaventure Cemetery. Southern Crosses of Honor on graves of Confederate soldiers signify loyalty and honorable service to the South. The United Daughters of the Confederacy created these.

5. Statue to Corinne E. Lawton

Civiletti Palermo made this monument in 1879. Legend has it that Corinne Lawton threw herself into the Savannah River to protest marrying a man she didn't love. Her back is to the river, symbolizing that she drowned. The wreath at her feet represents victory over death. Hint: Look for her in section H.

6. Nautical Angel Pointing Up

The Nautical Star this statue wears on her head symbolizes sea service. The anchor she is holding is a sign of hope or eternal life, and her single finger pointing up is a sign of leading the departed up to heaven.

Bonus Find

➤ The little angels on this tomb watch over their loved ones. The wings and clouds symbolize carrying the souls to heaven.

7. The Little Angel with the Seashell

This white marble monument is referred to as "The Baldwin Angel." Engraved over the little angel's head is Mark 10:15: *Verily I say unto you whosoever shall not receive the Kingdom of God as a little child he shall not enter therein.* The shell is a symbol of baptism and rebirth. Hint: Look behind the marble wall in section H.

8. Johnny Mercer's Bench

In the Mercer family plot is the bench memorial to Johnny Mercer, one of the most popular singers, songwriters, and lyricists of the twentieth century. He was born and raised in Savannah, and though he traveled the world, he came back to Savannah and was laid to rest in Bonaventure Cemetery.

Bonus Finds

➤ Read what is engraved on Johnny Mercer's headstone: *And the Angels Sing.*

➤ Find what is engraved on the headstone of Johnny Mercer's wife, Ginger: *Must Have Been a Beautiful Baby.*

9. The Lady with Flowers

Placing flowers on a gravesite is an act of remembering and celebrating those who are no longer with us. Roses are a symbol of love, respect, and courage.

10. The Mausoleums

The two famous mausoleums along Bonaventure Way hold the Schwalbe family and the Wessels family. It was a show of wealth to be buried above ground, and these tombs were meant to resemble small churches on the inside, with altars and stained-glass windows. It is beautiful when the sun shines through the stained glass and lights up each mausoleum.

Bonus Find

➤ Stand directly in front of the mausoleums and look toward the back to see the stained-glass windows.

11. The Draped Column

This is the grave of Antonio Aliffi, a popular Italian sculptor who was invited to come to Savannah in 1898 and work for sculptor John Walz. Walz owned a marble yard and created many of the beautiful monuments in Bonaventure Cemetery. Aliffi was reported to have worked on many of the monuments as well. He also carved on Georgia's Stone Mountain and Mount Rushmore in South Dakota. A broken column symbolizes mortality, and a draped column represents the divide between earthly life and heavenly life. Hint: Look in section K.

12. Winged Angel with Flowers

This angel is standing watch and holding flowers as a sign of celebration in life and death. Her large wings represent protection and the flight of souls to heaven.

Bonus Find

➤ Look for the two little cherubs over the family's initial, *W.*

13. The Theus Tomb

The Theus Tomb shows a grieving lady holding a wreath of flowers. Thomas N. Theus and his wife, Eliza, are buried beneath her. He was a Confederate soldier in the Chatham Artillery. Hint: Look in section H.

14. Draped Urns or Tree Trunks

You will see many draped urns and tree trunks throughout Bonaventure Cemetery. The urns represent the soul, and the cloth is a sign of mourning or the divide between earthly life and heavenly life. The tree trunks symbolize a life cut short. They usually display other symbols to tell about the person's life. How many urns and tree trunks can you find?

15. The Jewish Section of Bonaventure

The Jewish section was added in 1909. An archway marks the entrance. The Jewish faithful observe a mourning period of seven days, and on the one-year anniversary of the death, the final mourning ritual involves placing a stone on the grave as a sign of remembrance. Hint: Look in section Q, Sheftall Way.

Bonus Finds

➤ Look for a tomb that features flowers and a menorah. Roses are a sign of beauty and love, and daisies represent innocence. A menorah usually indicates that the deceased was a "righteous woman."

➤ Can you find the tree trunk with the Star of David? The size of the tree trunk indicates whether the person was young or elderly at the time of death.

Here are more things to look for in Bonaventure Cemetery and what they symbolize.

➤ A hand pointing down represents the hand of God descending from heaven. A scroll symbolizes the scriptures.

➤ A bird on a grave signifies peace and also represents a messenger of God. The most common birds on gravestones are doves.

➤ Lambs are often used on children's graves as a sign of innocence. A sleeping lamb is a Victorian symbol for death.

➤ An angel represents a guide to heaven. A hand pointing up reminds us that our loved ones are not here. Their souls are in heaven.

➤ The cross represents Christianity. The clasped hands symbolize unity and God greeting the deceased.

➤ An open Bible or book is often used on graves of clergymen or devoted religious people. An open book can also represent the Book of Life, noting a person's good deeds and accomplishments.

➤ An oak leaf symbolizes a long life.

> In Christianity, a crown and cross signify victory. A six-pointed star represents the Creation.

> An angel writes the names of the deceased in the Book of Life.

> A sleeping child is a Victorian symbol for death.

➤ Roses represent love and beauty.

➤ An Easter lily is a sign of purity, youth, and virtue. It is also a symbol associated with the Virgin Mary.

There are lots of things to find in Bonaventure Cemetery.

What were your favorite discoveries?

On the way to Tybee Island there is more. . . .

Take a left on President's Expressway and continue until it merges left onto U.S. 80. Follow U.S. 80 onto Tybee Island.

Bonus Find

➤ Old Fort Jackson is located on the Savannah River three miles east of the Historic District. It is the oldest fort in Georgia, and the site has been in use since the 1740s. Fort Jackson was fortified during the Revolutionary War, saw action during the War of 1812, and was the Confederate headquarters for defenses of the Savannah River during the Civil War. It was named for James Jackson, who came to Savannah in 1722 and fought in the Revolutionary War. He had the honor of accepting the surrender of the British in Savannah in 1782. Jackson was also the most famous duelist in Savannah. Today the Coastal Heritage Society operates the restored Old Fort Jackson.

Tybee Island

Tybee Island

Tybee Island, Georgia is eighteen miles east of Savannah. When you exit Thunderbolt, Victory Drive becomes U.S. 80 East, which ends on Tybee Island.

The History of Tybee Island

Tybee Island is the easternmost point in the state of Georgia. It is a barrier island right at the mouth of the Savannah River. Indians first inhabited the island, and *Tybee* is an Indian word for salt. Then came the Spaniards, French, and English, and let's not forget about the pirates who often visited the area. Tybee Island was used as a military outpost during the Revolutionary War, War of 1812, Civil War, Spanish-American War, World War I, and World War II. After the Civil War, the people of Savannah started to come here to escape the heat of the city, referring to it as "Savannah Beach." In 1887, the Central of Georgia Railroad completed a railway between Savannah and Tybee Island. In the 1920s, U.S. 80 was built, further connecting Tybee Island to the mainland. Today Tybee Island is a fun-loving, laidback beach community known for its Pirate Fest, St. Patrick's Day, and Mermaid and Beach Bum parades It has much to offer, with its beautiful beaches, barrier islands, historic homes, old forts, lighthouses, and perfect sunsets. So . . . ahoy, mateys. Let the treasure hunt begin!

1. Fort Pulaski

The fort was named for Gen. Casimir Pulaski and was built between 1829 and 1847 by the U.S. Army Corps of Engineers. Gen. Simon Bernard designed it, and Robert E. Lee devised the drainage system on his first assignment after graduating from West Point. The fort was constructed of Savannah gray bricks, red bricks, sandstone, and granite from England. Its walls are seven and a half feet thick and were thought to be indestructible. In 1862, after Georgia troops seized the fort, Union forces used a new type of cannon against it, a rifled cannon that fired elongated and pointed projectiles rather than round balls. These new cannons did major damage to Fort Pulaski and forced the Confederate troops to surrender after thirty hours of heavy bombardment. Today Fort Pulaski is operated by the National Park Service and open to the public. They have cannon firings daily!

2. Rails to Trails

Rails to Trails is part of the old railroad line that the Central of Georgia Railroad built between Savannah and Tybee Island in 1887. It has been turned into a six-mile nature trail today, running through McQueen's Island. It also runs along the mouth of the Savannah River and the entryway to the port of Savannah. It is a great nature trail for hikers, runners, or bikers through the saltwater marshes and over bridges, with lots of discoveries to be made! Keep your eyes open for dolphins in the river, box turtles, marsh rabbits, osprey, red-tailed hawks, brown pelicans, crabs, American alligators, and many different types of snakes.

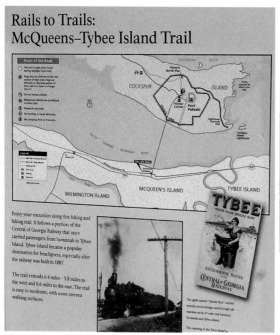

3. The Cockspur Island Lighthouse

The Cockspur Island Lighthouse was built in 1848 by John Norris, a New York architect who also constructed the Andrew Low House and Greene-Meldrim House. It is located twelve miles east of the port of Savannah, right at the mouth of the Savannah River. This little lighthouse has survived many hurricanes, floods, fires, and the Union attack on Fort Pulaski during the Civil War. It operated until June 1, 1909, and in 1958 the U.S. Coast Guard transferred it to the National Park Service. The Cockspur Island Lighthouse is open to the public but hard to get to unless you have a boat. The best way to view it is from the overlook trail at the end of Rails to Trails.

The Cockspur Island Lighthouse is where "The Waving Girl," Florence Martus, waved at all the ships entering or leaving the port.

4. "Welcome Tybee Island" Sign

This is a popular photo spot for visitors!

5. Tybee Island Anchor

This anchor was found off the north shore of Tybee Island. It was pulled up from the wreckage of a sunken wooden sailing ship. Thought to date to around 1849, it was discovered and brought in by Capt. Bill Walsh. With the Atlantic Ocean in the background, this is also a great spot for photos!

6. Tybee Memorial Cemetery

This is the only cemetery on Tybee Island. The first burial took place in the early 1870s. Many of the people interred here were victims of drowning or shipwrecks. A plaque states: *Much of its history remains shrouded in mystery.*

TYBEE MEMORIAL CEMETERY

Bonus Find

➤ Look for the ship on the playground. Hint: It is located between the Tybee Library and Tybee Memorial Cemetery.

7. Tybee Island Pier and Pavilion

The original Tybee Island Pier was built in 1891 by the Central of Georgia Railroad and was named the Tybrisa. It stood for many years as a landmark on the Atlantic Ocean. It became popular with families coming for the day and with seasonal visitors. With its open dancefloor, it became a regular stop for touring big bands. Sadly, a fire destroyed it in 1967. The pier and pavilion you see today were built in 1996 and are still a popular site with visitors!

Bonus Find

> ➤ Look for the mural of sea creatures.

8. Tybee Island Marine Science Center

The Tybee Island Marine Science Center is a great place to go to learn more about coastal Georgia! Open from 10:00 to 5:00 daily, it offers beach walks, marsh treks, and day sea camps for kids.

Its mission is to "cultivate a responsible stewardship of coastal Georgia's natural resources through education, conservation, and research."

9. The Dolphin Fountain

This fountain is located in the Park of Seven Flags, named for the seven flags that have flown over Tybee Island. The Spanish came in 1520, then the French in 1605. The pirate flag is a reminder of the chaotic period in Tybee's history before the English founded the colony in 1733. The British flag, the "King's Colors," flew until the Revolutionary War. After the war, the Georgia state flag and the American flag flew over Tybee Island. In 1861, the flag of the Confederacy replaced the American flag. After General Sherman's "March to the Sea" in 1864, the American flag was reinstated. Today we have the current Georgia state flag, adopted in 2003.

Bonus Find

➤ At the east end of U.S. 80, look for the signs marking the terminus of the original 1926 route.

10. The Tybee Island Lighthouse

The first lighthouse was built in 1736. It was ninety feet tall and said to be the tallest structure in the country at that time. When it was destroyed by a storm, a second lighthouse replaced it in 1742. That was also destroyed by a storm and rebuilt in 1773, but in 1862, Confederate soldiers burned the interior so Union troops could not use it. It was repaired after the war with a first-order Fresnel lens. George Jackson was the last on-site lighthouse keeper. After his death in 1948, the U.S. Coast Guard took over operating and maintaining the lighthouse. The lighthouse was restored in 1999, and today the Tybee Island Historical Society maintains it as a museum.

Bonus Find

➤ Count the stairs to the top of the lighthouse. How many are there? You can see the whole island from the top!

11. Tybee Island Museum

This museum is located in one of the fortifications of Fort Screven. This fort was one of the largest on the Atlantic coast. It was built in 1875, located on the mouth of the Savannah River on Tybee Island. The U.S. government placed heavy batteries here before the Spanish-American War, facing the channel. Coastal artillery units manned the large guns during World Wars I and II. In 1946, the government declared the site to be surplus property. You can see sections of this old fort from all over the north side of Tybee Island. The Tybee Island Historical Society owns the Tybee Island Museum, which provides a deeper look into Tybee's history and the people who have shaped it through the years. There are so many things to discover inside, and there is also a nice view of the beach from the top of the fort!

12. Little Tybee Island

Little Tybee Island is accessible only by boat, but you can see it from the south end of Tybee Island. It is actually two times bigger than Tybee Island. Little Tybee Island is mostly saltmarsh with pristine beaches and forests of pine, live oak, and palm trees. It is between Williamson Island at its southern end and Wassaw Island just four miles away. The state of Georgia owns and protects Little Tybee as an unspoiled, uninhabited wilderness preserve. It is home to dolphins, raccoons, minks, gray foxes, feral pigs, deer, and alligators. It is also a nesting spot for many birds, including bald eagles.

A fun way to get to Little Tybee is by paddleboard!

Bonus Finds on Tybee Island

➤ How many pirate flags can you find? There are legends that some pirate treasures were never found and are still buried on one of these barrier islands.

➤ How many sea turtles can you see, either real or manmade? These fascinating creatures come onto the beach in March through October to lay and bury their eggs. Tybee Island is a popular nesting spot for sea turtles. Be very careful not to disturb any nests!

➤ How many surfboards can you count? Hot Sushi's Happy Surf Camp Aloha! is a great way to learn to surf on Tybee Island!

There are many good family-friendly finds for lunch or dinner on Tybee. The Crab Shack is a popular one.

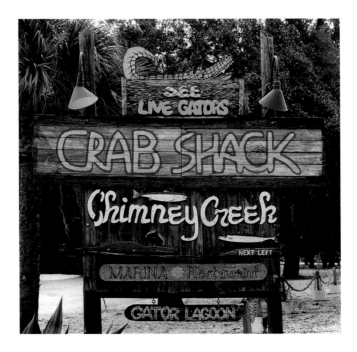

Bonus Find

➤ Look for the alligator lagoon at the Crab Shack.

There are so many things to discover on Tybee Island.

What were your favorite Tybee Island finds?

What discovery surprised you the most?

What were your favorite memories?

It's sad, I know, but now that your Savannah scavenger hunt has come to a close . . .

Which search was your favorite?

What was your best find?

What did you find that wasn't in this book?

And if you didn't find them all, there is always next time. . . .

This page is for your photos, drawings, and memories of your discoveries.

The world is full of treasures. What can you find?

Acknowledgments

I am very grateful to

➤ my family and friends for supporting me

➤ the Owens-Thomas House for inspiring the idea for this book

➤ the Georgia Historical Society, Tybee Historical Society, Bonaventure Historical Society, Historic Savannah Foundation, and Savannah Area Chamber of Commerce

Answer Key and Information

Historic Downtown Savannah

Leopold's Ice Cream is at 212 East Broughton Street, between Abercorn Street and Lincoln Street. For more information, call 912-234-4442 or go to www.leopoldsicecream.com.

1. Forsyth Park starts at the intersection of Bull Street and Gaston Street. The fountain is right at the front, and if you keep walking down the middle of Forsyth Park, heading south past the playgrounds, you can see the Confederate Monument in the center.

Bonus Finds: The Fragrant Garden is located behind the big playground to the right as you face south coming into Forsyth Park. The three fauns holding up a bench are at the back of the garden, under the covered area. The Fragrant Garden is open from 9:00 to 2:00 on weekdays except holidays.

2. The Cathedral of Saint John the Baptist is at the intersection of Abercorn Street and Harris Street, on Lafayette Square.

Bonus Finds: The stained-glass window of Saint Patrick is the fourth one on the right as you come into the church. The saints are on parade at the very top, on the right and left above the main aisle. Saint Denis is on the right side as you face the altar, in the fifth group of saints. Saint Joan of Arc is also on the right, in the first group. The Cathedral of Saint John the Baptist is open daily from 8:00 to 5:00. It is closed for 12:00 o'clock mass during the week and Sunday mass in the morning. It is a popular wedding church here in Savannah, so it can be hard to get in on Saturdays. For more information, call 912-233-4709.

3. The Andrew Low House is at 329 Abercorn Street, on the right side of Lafayette Square if you are heading south. For more information, call 912-232-6854 or check them out at www.andrewlowhouse.com or on Facebook.

4. Bonus Find: The Unitarian Universalist Church is at 321 Habersham Street, on the right side of Troup Square if you are facing south. For more information, call 912-234-0980.

5. The monument to Sgt. William Jasper is in the middle of Madison Square, on Bull Street between Harris and Charlton streets.

Bonus Finds: Saint John's Episcopal Church is at 1 West Macon Street, on the southwest corner of Madison Square. For more info, go to www.stjohnssav.org. The cannons are on either side of the main entrance of the Savannah Volunteer Guards Armory, at 340-344 Bull Street on the southeast corner of Madison Square. The Scottish Rite Temple is located at 341 Bull Street.

6. Jones Street runs east-west between Charlton Street and Taylor Street. Mrs. Wilkes' Dining Room is at 107 West Jones Street and Whitaker Street. It is open weekdays from 11:00 to 2:00. For more information, call 912-232-5997.

7. Massie School is on the southwest side of Calhoun Square, at Abercorn Street and East Taylor Street. For more information, call 912-395-5070 or check out www.massieschool.com.

8. Congregation Mickve Israel is on the southeast corner of Monterey Square, at 20 East Gordon Street. The synagogue is open for tours during the week from 10:00 to 1:00 and 2:00 to 4:00. For more information, call 912-233-1547 or go to www.mickveisrael.org.

Bonus Find: The Casimir Pulaski Monument is in the center of Monterey Square.

9. Colonial Park Cemetery's front gates are at the intersection of Abercorn Street and Oglethorpe Avenue.

Bonus Finds: Button Gwinnett's monument is close to the front gates, in the middle; look for the large memorial with four columns. There are many snakes represented throughout this cemetery. The largest one is to the right of the Button Gwinnett monument. The skull and crossbones may be found on a broken headstone mounted on the wall at the back of the cemetery. Colonial Park Cemetery is open daily from 8:00 to 8:00.

10. The Owens-Thomas House is on the east side of Oglethorpe Square at 124 Abercorn Street. For more information, call 912-233-9743 or check out www.telfair.org.

Bonus Finds: The cast-iron balcony is on the right side of the Owens-Thomas House, facing East President Street. As you walk to Columbia Square, the orange-tree gate is on East York Street, on the side of 123 Habersham Street.

11. Columbia Square Fountain is in the middle of the square.

Bonus Find: The cast-iron frogs are at the bottom of the fountain, on either side of the roots. There are four of them.

12. The Davenport House is located at 324 East State Street. For more information, call 912-236-8097 or go to www.davenporthousemuseum.org.

Bonus Find: The Davenport House's English Garden is behind and to the left of the home.

13. The Pirate's House is at 20 East Broad Street. For more information, call 912-233-5757 or check out www.thepirateshouse.com.

Bonus Finds: The Herb House is on the right side of the Pirate's House, of which it is a part today. The tunnels and rum cellar are under the restaurant's main dining area.

14. "The Waving Girl" statue is on the east end of River Street, past all the shops.

15. City Hall is at 2 East Bay Street.

Bonus Finds: The "Washington Guns" are on the east side of City Hall facing Bay Street. The griffin is in front of the Cotton Exchange, located at 201 East River Street.

16. The monument to Nathanael Greene is in the middle of Johnson Square, the first square on Bull Street heading south from the river.

Bonus Find: Christ Church Episcopal is on the southeast corner of Johnson Square. For more information, go to www. christchurchsavannah.org.

17. The First African Baptist Church is near Franklin Square at 23 Montgomery Street. For more information, check out www.firstafricanbc.com.

Bonus Finds: Ellis Square is the first square on Barnard Street heading south from the river. Paula Deen's Lady and Sons Restaurant is on the corner of West Congress Street and Whitaker Street. For more information, call 912-233-2600 or go to www.ladyandsons.com.

18. Telfair Art Museum is located at 121 Barnard Street. For more information, call 912-790-8800 or check out www. telfair.org.

Bonus Finds: The Jepson Center is on the southwest corner of Telfair Square. For more information, call 912-790-8800 or go to www.telfair.org/visit/jepson.

19. Tomochichi's Grave and the Gordon Monument are in the middle of Wright Square, on Bull Street between East State Street and East York Street.

Bonus Finds: The boulder in honor of Tomochichi is in the southeast corner of Wright Square. The train is engraved on the east side of the Gordon Monument. The face on the U.S. Federal Building, located at 125 Bull Street, is on the West York Street side. It is in the middle of the building on the second floor.

20. Independent Presbyterian Church is at 207 Bull Street.

Bonus Finds: The Juliette Gordon Low birthplace is at 10 East Oglethorpe Avenue. The garden is on the east side of the house. For more information, call 912-233-4501 or check out www.juliettegordonlowbirthplace.org. The "ladies" are over the side entrance to the Old Chatham Academy, 208 Bull Street.

21. Chippewa Square is the third square on Bull Street heading south from the river. It is between East Hull Street and East Perry Street.

Bonus Find: Savannah Theatre is on the northeast corner of Chippewa Square at 222 Bull Street. For more information, call 912-233-7764 or go to www.savannahtheatre.com.

22. Georgia State Railroad Museum is located at 655 Louisville Road. For more information, call 912-651-6823 or check out www.chsgeorgia.org.

Bonus Find: The Savannah Children's Museum is at the same location. For more information, call 912-651-4292 or go to www.savannahchildrensmuseum.org.

Bonaventure Cemetery

1. The two front gates at Bonaventure Cemetery, the Christian Gate and the Jewish Gate, are at 330 Bonaventure Road. The Christian entrance is on the left and the Jewish entrance is on the right behind the Bonaventure Administrative Building. All the graves are well marked, and maps and markers are posted throughout the cemetery, online, and at the main office. For more information, check out www. bonaventurehistorical.org.

2. The Gaston Tomb is just inside the main entrance of the cemetery, directly in front of the Christian entrance to the right.

3. The Little Gracie statue is in section E, lot 99.

Bonus find: The angel with the palm branch is directly to the left of Little Gracie.

4. The Bust of Gen. Robert H. Anderson is in section F, lot 12.

Bonus Find: This Confederate sword is in section F, lot 20. This Confederate hat and sash can be found in section H, lot 75.

5. The statue to Corinne E. Lawton is in section H, lot 166, 167, at the back of the cemetery overlooking the Wilmington River.

6. The nautical angel pointing up is in section E, across from the Lawton lots.

Bonus find: The little angels tomb is right behind it, in section H, lot 87.

7. The little angel with the seashell is in the Baldwin plot in section H, lot 39. She has a curved, white marble wall around her and is facing away from the cemetery.

8. Johnny Mercer's bench and grave are in section H, lot 48.

9. The lady with flowers is in section H, lot 33.

10. These two mausoleums are in section A. The Schwalbe family mausoleum is in lot 238, and the Wessels family mausoleum is in lot 165.

11. The draped column is in section K, lot 376.

12. The angel with the large wings and flowers is in section C, lot 6.

Bonus Find: The two little cherubs over the family's initial W are below and to the left of the statue of the lady placing flowers on a grave. They are in section C, lot 6.

13. The Theus Tomb is in section H, lot 30.

14. Some examples of draped urns may be found in section C, down Wiltberger Way. This tree trunk is in section K, lot 302.

15. Bonus Finds: The tomb with the flowers and menorah is

behind the Jewish archway, to the left side. The tree trunk with the Star of David is at the beginning of aisle Q7, on the right side.

Bonus Find: To drive to Old Fort Jackson from Savannah's Historic District, starting at President Street at Houston Street, head east on President Street for about two miles. Then take a left onto Woodcock Road. Go half a mile and take the first right, onto Fort Jackson Road. The address is 1 Fort Jackson Road. For more information, call 912-232-3945 or go to www.chsgeorgia.org.

More things to look for in Bonaventure Cemetery: The hand pointing down is in section A, lot 235. The bird is in section E, lot 48. The lambs are in section C, lots 33 and 34. The angel pointing up is in section C along Noble Jones Drive. The two hands with the cross are in section C, lot 34, along Wiltberger Way. The Bible or book is in section H, lot 55. The grave with the oak leaf is in section C, lot 33. The crosses are in section E, lot 107. The angel writing in the Book of Life is in section N, lot 84. The sleeping children are in section N, lot 84. The Easter lilies are in section H, lot 62. The roses on the grave are in section F, lot 20.

Tybee Island

1. Fort Pulaski is on U.S. 80, heading east to Tybee Island, just before the Cockspur Island Lighthouse. It is open daily from 9:00 to 5:00. For more information, call 912-786-5787 or go to www.nps.gov/fopu.

2. Rails to Trails runs along U.S. 80 east through McQueen's Island headed toward Tybee Island. There is an entrance to the trail on the left side of the gates going into Fort Pulaski. For more information, check out www.railstotrails.us.

3. The Cockspur Island Lighthouse is part of the Fort Pulaski National Monument. For more information, call 912-786-5787 or go to www.nps.gov/fopu.

4. The "Welcome Tybee Island" sign on U.S. 80 may be seen as you head east toward Tybee Island. Just over the Lazaretto Creek Bridge and past the Cockspur Island Lighthouse, look to the right.

5. The Tybee Island anchor is on Butler Avenue, on the left side of the curve just before Second Street, in Kullman Park.

6. Tybee Memorial Cemetery is at 403 Butler Avenue, behind the Tybee Island Library.

7. Tybee Island Pier and Pavilion are just off U.S. 80 at the end of Tybrisa Street.

Bonus Find: The mural of sea creatures is on the right side of the Tybee Island Pier and Pavilion, facing Seventeenth Street.

8. The Tybee Island Marine Science Center is at 1509 Strand Avenue. For more information, call 912-786-5917 or check out www.TybeeMarineScience.org.

9. The Park of Seven Flags is at Butler Avenue and Tybrisa Street.

Bonus Find: The end of U.S. 80 signs are in front of the Park of Seven Flags.

10. The Tybee Island Lighthouse is eighteen miles east of Savannah. At the first stoplight on Tybee Island, take a left on Campbell Avenue, which deadends at Van Horne Street. Take a left onto Van Horne Street, then take a right on Meddin Drive. Stay on Meddin Drive until you see the Tybee Island Lighthouse at 30 Meddin Drive. It is open from 9:00 to 5:30, every day except Tuesday. (They stop selling tickets at 4:30.) For more information, call 912-786-5801 or go to www.tybeelighthouse.org.

Bonus Find: There are 178 stairs.

11. The Tybee Island Museum is right across the street from the Tybee Island Lighthouse. Look for the seven flags in front of the museum. For more information, call 912-786-5801 or check out www.tybeelighthouse.org.

12. You can see Little Tybee Island from the south end of Tybee Island on Eighteenth Street.

For more information on Hot Sushi's Happy Surf Camp Aloha!, call 912-604-9527 or check them out at www.happy-surfing.info or on Facebook.

Board Loft, at 406 U.S. 80, is a great place to rent surfboards and paddleboards! For more information, call 912-472-4197 or go to www.boardloft.com.

North Island Surf and Kayak offers eco-tours, surf lessons, and rentals! For more information, call 912-786-4000 or check out www.northislandkayak.com.

Captain Mike's Dolphin Tours offers sunset cruises. For more information, call 912-786-5848 or go to www.tybeedolphins. com.

The Crab Shack is located at 40 Estill Hammock Road. For more information, call 912-786-9857 or go to www. thecrabshack.com.

Index